THE
SUICIDE RAID

THE CANADIANS AT DIEPPE
AUGUST 19TH, 1942

by

N. M. Christie

Access to History No. 5

CEF BOOKS
2001

D0107520

Canadian Cataloguing in Publication Data
Christie, N.M.
    The suicide raid: the Canadians at Dieppe, 1942
(Access to history series; no. 5)
Includes bibliographical references.
ISBN 1-896979-36-X
    1. Dieppe Raid, 1942. I. Title. II. Series: Access to History series; no. 5.

D756.5.D5C48   2001 940.54'21425   C00-901677-5

Published by:
    CEF BOOKS
    PO BOX 40083,
    OTTAWA, ONTARIO K1V 0W8
    613-823-7000

This book is dedicated to the memory of the 110,000 Canadians who willingly gave their lives in the defence of freedom in the Twentieth Century.

Lest We Forget

Acknowledgements:
    We would like to thank Ontario Command of The Royal Canadian Legion and the Department of Canadian Heritage for the support which made this series possible. Additional thanks to Mr. Brian McClean, Dr. Hugh Henry, Mr. Tim Stewart and Mr. Rob Linden for their valuable contributions to this book.

Publication of this book has been supported by the Canadian War Museum.

September 4, 1942

Dear Mrs. Tucker:-

This is to inform you that your Husband was reported "Missing" following the great raid on Dieppe on the 19th of August 1942.

Just as soon as any additional information is to hand you may rest assured that you will be informed by the proper authorities.

The undersigned joins the Commanding Officer and all other members of the Regiment in sharing with you the natural anxieties at this time. We are proud of the men of the Battalion who fought so well in this engagement and know that their noble sacrifice has already meant much to the ultimate triumph of the Allied Nations.

With Sincere Sympathy
I remain John Hodgson,
Chaplain, Royal Regiment of Canada

Of the 554 men of the Royal Regiment of Canada who went on the Dieppe Raid, only 65 returned.

FRANÇAIS!

Ceci est un coup de main et non pas l'invasion.

Nous vous prions instamment de n'y prendre part en aucune façon et de ne faire quoi que ce soit qui puisse entraîner des représailles de la part de l'ennemi.

Nous faisons appel à votre sang-froid et à votre bon sens.

Lorsque l'heure sonnera, nous vous avertirons. C'est alors que nous agirons côte-à-côte pour notre victoire commune et pour votre liberté !

The leaflet dropped by Allied aircraft over Dieppe. It reads:
"It is a helping hand not an invasion. We pray do not take part in any way or do anything that could bring retribution from the enemy. We ask you to be calm and use common sense. When the time comes we will tell you. It is then that we will act side-by-side for our common victory and your freedom." (Tim Stewart Collection)

Table of Contents

FORTRESS EUROPE - JUNE 1943

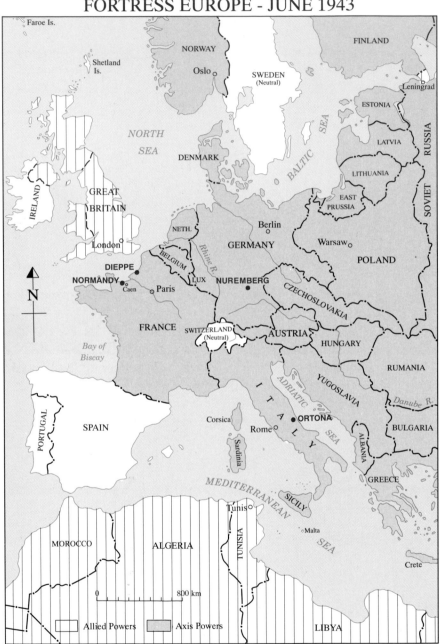

Introduction

In the early morning of Wednesday, August 19th, 1942, a 200 vessel convoy containing 5,000 Canadian troops approached the French port of Dieppe. In the next few hours the Canadian force would be destroyed. The bodies of more than 900 Canadian men would be scattered along the water front and their vessels and equipment left burning and smouldering on the blood-stained beaches.

The Dieppe Raid is one of the most bitter and controversial episodes in Canadian history. That it is Canada's worst military disaster is beyond doubt. But what makes the sacrifice more painful is the lingering question - was it worth it? Were the "lessons" learned from the failure of the Dieppe Raid critical to the Allied victories later in the war or were the important "lessons" strictly a cover-up by the Generals of a poorly planned and poorly executed operation?

To understand the Dieppe Raid it is necessary to see the world as it was in 1942. The Second World War had been raging for three years and it appeared that Germany and its Axis allies would win. Since 1939 Hitler's armies had conquered all of Europe and inflicted major defeats on the soldiers of the British Empire in France, Norway, Greece, Crete and North Africa. German submarines were sinking Allied shipping seemingly at will. In 1941 Russia was forced into the war on Britain's side, but the seemingly invincible German Army smashed Joseph Stalin's huge but inefficient Soviet Red Army. Within six months the Nazis were at the gates of Moscow. The Soviets had suffered terribly, and were desperate for assistance. They needed the British (and at the end of 1941, also the United States) to relieve some of the overpowering German pressure and start a Second Front by invading Europe.

It was out of this desperation that the original plan for a major raid on the port of Dieppe was created. Decisions made in desperation are rarely good ones; but the Soviets had to have the support. Without it, maybe they too would fall under the heels of Adolf Hitler's advancing hordes.

Canadian troops had been in England since 1939 but had not seen any action. By 1942 all the other members of the British Empire, Australians, New Zealanders, Indians and South Africans, had played important roles in big battles, and showed themselves to be good fighters. For the

Canadians, the monotony and maybe even the embarrassment of others doing their fighting for them prompted them to push for involvement in the upcoming Raid.

It was for these reasons the ships were packed with Canadian soldiers on their way to a small port on the Normandy coast. Their success on the beaches would depend on planning, firepower, and surprise. One thing that no one had to worry about was the tenacity and courage of the men in the convoy, for they were the sons of the Conquerors of Vimy.

Troops of the Cameron Highlanders of Canada in Landing Craft prior to the raid on Dieppe.   (PAC-113245)

The World at War 1939 to 1942

It is difficult today to understand how close the war was to being lost in those early years. When war was declared in 1939 it was essentially a European conflict, pitting France and the British Empire against the fascist countries of Germany and Italy. The first eight months of the war were so quiet it was known as the "phony war" as the opposing armies faced each other along the French-German frontier. Two of the world's strongest powers, the Soviet Union and the United States, were neutral.

The entire war changed in May 1940. Nazi Germany launched a massive attack on the French, and using rapid deployment of armour, particularly tanks, routed the French Army and forced the retreating British Army to evacuate the continent and return to England. In June 1940 France surrendered. The Germans had already captured Holland, Belgium, Denmark, and Norway. Now Nazi Germany was the master of Europe.

Britain and its Empire, including Canada, Australia, India and New Zealand, stood alone against Hitler's seemingly invincible armies. In the summer and fall of 1940 Britain prepared for the next assault. Canadian troops were rushed overseas to form an important part of the backbone for the defence of the British Isles, and the "Battle of Britain" raged in the skies over England. With bated breath they awaited the sightings of the armada that would signal the sea-born German invasion. It never came.

Gradually the war spread into North Africa and the Mediterranean; but as they had in France and Norway, the Germans inflicted major defeats on the British and Commonwealth forces in Greece, Crete and North Africa. German submarines were prowling the Atlantic Ocean sinking British shipping. It appeared to everyone that the war was lost, that the fascist tyrant, Adolf Hitler would dominate the world.

In June 1941 Hitler made one of two crucial mistakes that would cost Germany the war. The Nazis invaded the then neutral Soviet Union, widening the war, and taking on an enemy so massive that German resources would be stretched to the breaking point. Hitler's decision gave Britain breathing space and another ally.

As had happened in Europe the nightmare continued with the Nazi Wermacht slicing through the Russian forces, capturing millions of prisoners. In less than six months they had advanced 1,000 km, and were at the gates of Moscow. This incredible advance caught the Soviets completely off-guard and for a time it seemed like they were beaten. A harsh winter stopped the German advance, and the Russians had until the spring of 1942 to regroup. Needless to say they asked for as much help as they could from Britain. The main war was now being fought on Russian soil and a "Second Front" was needed, to pull German reserves away from Russia.

If the British Empire (Commonwealth) thought things could not get worse they were wrong. On December 7, 1941 the Japanese, Germany's Axis ally, attacked the British and American forces in the Far East at Pearl Harbor, Hong Kong, Malaya, Singapore, and the Philippines. In a few short months the Japanese had conquered them all and had captured tens of thousands of American, British, Australian, Canadian* and Indian troops. They were rapidly advancing into Burma and towards Australia. The Japanese seemed as invincible as the Nazis. The Rising Sun dominated Asia, like the Swastika ruled Europe.

By the spring of 1942 the world was aflame. British defeats, Russian defeats and American defeats had crushed the morale of the people. The Allies had to hold on or all would be lost.

The Atlantic Wall

In 1941 the Germans had abandoned their plan to invade Britain. They were now fighting on two fronts, in North Africa and in Soviet Russia, where the majority of their armies were engaged. Hitler decided to hold Western Europe in a defensive mode. He knew any invasion would have to be by sea and would have to come within a practical distance from the British coast. The odds were it would also be on an established port because without a port it would be very difficult for the Allies to reinforce any landing. Consequently the Germans went about fortifying the major harbours along the Channel coast. Using the natural feature of steep chalk cliffs, known as the falaise, they tunnelled in, building complexes of bunkers for machine guns, and artillery. The bunkers were so effectively built that only a direct hit would cause any damage at all. This system of defence was selected to provide a maximum concentration of fire on the approaches to the port. Huge concrete tank blocks were built on any routes

*At Hong Kong in December 1941 the Japanese had killed or captured an entire Canadian force of 1,973 men. It was the Canadian Army's first foray in the war and they had suffered 100% casualties.

into the town itself. The beaches were also mined and wired. Each port along the Pas-de-Calais (the closest ports to Britain), from which you could see England, was built into an impregnable fortress. Further south along the Normandy coast the harbours were not as heavily fortified, but still presented fearsome defences. One of those fortified ports was the pleasant tourist haven of Dieppe.

The only small weaknesses in the German defences were the use of lower quality troops garrisoning the coastal region and limited air support. The war in Russia was finally taking a toll on the Germans' ability to fight.

Canada at War, 1939 to 1942

Canada had declared war on Germany on September 10, 1939. As had happened at the outbreak of war in 1914, Canadians had rushed to join the Colours. Their motives for enlisting were as varied as they had been twenty-five years before: patriotism, adventure, and after the Great Depression, three square meals a day and a job. Even knowing the catastrophic losses and deplorable conditions of the First World War did not deter the men from enlisting. This showed the remarkable courage of these volunteers. Canada's Permanent Army was small and woefully under-equipped, but was none-the-less game for the great adventure.

Before long Canadian troops were being shipped to England. By the end of 1940 there were 57,000 Canadians guarding the coast of the British Isles. In many ways they were the only real army there to prevent the German invasion. Canadians continued to arrive, but as the possibility of a Nazi attack waned their role as guardians became less and less important. Bored with garrison duty, and aware of the desperate need for fighting troops, the Canadians wanted action. They had stood by and watched as the other members of the Commonwealth fought with distinction: the Australians, Indians and Africans in North Africa and the New Zealanders in Crete. (Not all serving Canadians were idle, thousands were seeing action in the Air Force, Navy and Merchant Marine.)

Finally in May 1942 the Canadians got their orders. The Second Canadian Division was to participate in a major raid on an unknown seaport on the French coast.

The Second Front

In 1942 the Germans had continued their offensives in Russia. They steam-rolled the Soviets as easily as they had in 1941, capturing tens of thousands of prisoners, and advancing with ease. Nazi Army Groups were closing-in on the Russian oil reserves in the Caucus, and there was fighting in the outskirts of the Russian industrial city called Stalingrad. If 1941 had looked bad, 1942 looked even worse. Joseph Stalin, the Soviet leader, demanded his Allies, Britain and the United States, open a Second Front in western Europe. Winston Churchill, the Prime Minister of Britain and Franklin Roosevelt, the President of the United States knew mounting a Second Front was a huge undertaking that would take time. To pacify Stalin they gave him equipment, supplies and the assurance to launch a Second Front as early as possible. One of the political offerings to Stalin was an attack on a French port. The Raid was code-named Operation "Rutter".

Operation "Rutter"

Operation "Rutter" was mounted for many reasons, most of them political in nature: satisfying the Soviets, giving Canadians a taste of battle, and boosting morale at home. There was mounting pressure on the Home Front for action. Public rallies were demanding the British Government do something to help the Russians. Giving the Germans a bloody-nose at Dieppe would satisfy all of the above.

There were also a few real military reasons for the Raid. When the time came for the Allied invasion of western Europe they would have to capture a viable port quickly, before the Germans could destroy it, and hold it against all counter-attacks. Could this be done? There was some debate as to how well fortified these ports were and how the logistics of crossing the Channel would affect a co-ordinated amphibious assault. Could the Germans be surprised? Plus, the Allies needed experience in amphibious operations. "Rutter" could provide that experience. Thus the operation could offer something of military value.

The plan for "Rutter" was a complex one, using heavy bombers and the big guns of the ships of the Royal Navy to soften up the Nazi positions overlooking the beaches. Glider-born troops and paratroopers would be used to neutralize the large German artillery guns protecting the approaches to the port. Assaulting waves of infantry and tanks would then sweep into the town and beyond. They would hold their positions and finally make a tactical withdrawal to their awaiting landing craft and be gone. This was a very ambitious plan, utilizing resources that were just not readily available in 1942.

The infantry that was to be used to sweep across the beaches and seize the port was the inexperienced Second Canadian Division. To make up for their lack of actual experience its 18,000 men were specially trained in amphibious operations for the upcoming "show". They trained for three months until July 1942, when they were given the "Green light". The Show was on.

The Show's Off

In July 1942 the men of the Second Division went to their assigned embarkation points and were "sealed" into their vessels. It was at this point they learned their target would be Dieppe. Over the next few days they waited to ship out, but the weather would not cooperate. Finally on July 7, 1942 Operation "Rutter" was cancelled. The Show was off, and the Canadians returned to their dreary lives as the Guardians of the English Coast.

The Show's On; Operation "Jubilee"

In one of the most controversial episodes of the Dieppe Raid, Operation "Rutter" was revived and renamed Operation "Jubilee". Even after all these years it is still unclear exactly how this occurred and on whose authorization the Raid was remounted. The target was to remain Dieppe. (The Canadian soldiers were not informed of this until the day before the Raid. Their officers knew 10 days before.) Normally when an operation was remounted its destination was changed for security reasons. At least 10,000 people knew Dieppe was the original objective in July, and although it was likely German spies in England had found out this information, the High Command did not consider it a security risk. (To this day many Dieppe veterans feel the Germans had advanced knowledge of the Raid.)

"...when they got us on the boats again (we were told), we're going back to Dieppe. Well ... you could've heard a pin drop."
Bill Oliver, Private, Royal Regiment of Canada

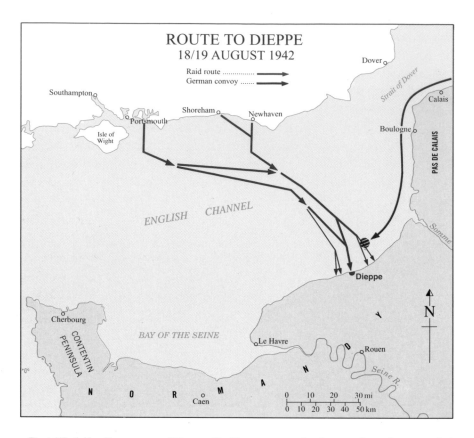

ROUTE TO DIEPPE
18/19 AUGUST 1942

But "Jubilee" was not "Rutter". Gone were the heavy bombers and the Royal Navy ships who would pound the port's defences, protect the infantry from counter-attacks, and cover the evacuation. Gone were the gliders and paratroopers. They were replaced by commandos. But what was going to take the place of the bombers and heavy guns? It appears the element of surprise and fighter coverage would have to do the trick. This was not a healthy trade-off.

The German Defences at Dieppe

Dieppe was chosen because it was a port within fighter range of England (100 km), and had beaches suitable for landing. The Allied planners felt it was not heavily defended (although many reports said all Channel ports had been converted into quasi-fortresses). Perhaps the fact it was further south along the French coast in Normandy, meant it would not be as well fortified as the ports in the Pas-de-Calais.

Dieppe is a port that has its own natural defences. Its 1.6 km beach is flanked by steep, unscalable chalk cliffs. From the cliffs, known as the East and West Headlands, the defender has those on the beach at his mercy. It was on these Headlands that the Nazis built their machine gun and artillery emplacements and behind the cliffs mortar posts were built so the mortars could safely lob shells onto the beaches. From these well protected positions the Germans could quickly bring a murderous concentration of fire onto the invaders.

The Germans had used these natural features and had simply exploited them by adding concrete pillboxes, barbed wire and large cement road blocks (preventing access to the town itself). In addition there was plenty of artillery available for support, including 41 guns and howitzers. Their arsenal also included three anti-aircraft batteries and 9 anti-tank guns. There were also 3,000 German troops garrisoning Dieppe and the surrounding coast.

Because the conditions of the moon and tides are so critical in the success of sea-born operations, the Germans were in a state of special alert between August 10/11 and August 19/20, when the conditions favoured a landing.

The Plan - Operation "Jubilee"

Operation "Jubilee" involved the military forces embarking from five ports along the "English coast"; Southampton, Gosport, Portsmouth, Shoreham and Newhaven. The force itself consisted of 4,963 Canadian soldiers (infantry, machine gunners, engineers, tank crews, etc.), 1,057 British Commandos and 50 United States Rangers (the first action for an American unit in Europe). The convoy totalled 253 vessels and was manned by 3,000 sailors of the Royal Navy and the Royal Canadian Navy.

The plan called for five separate attacks along 16 km of the Normandy coast. The principal assault would be on Dieppe. The four others were subsidiary flank attacks.

The Flank Attacks

The flank attacks were to be delivered simultaneously, in "nautical twilight" at 4:50 A.M. They would rely on surprise. The main attack would come 30 minutes later.

The Commandos

Two separate British Commando units would attack coastal batteries. On the extreme west of the attack: No.4 Commando would assault coastal batteries near Varengeville, and on the extreme east No.3 Commando was assigned the task of eliminating a German battery near Berneval. These operations were designed to protect the approaches to the main attack, but were not directly linked to the main frontal assault on Dieppe.

The other two flanking attacks were to be made by Canadian troops, on villages just 2 km east (Puys) and just 4 km west (Pourville) of Dieppe. They had a crucial role in the success of the main assault. The responsibility of these troops was to secure the cliffs (East and West Headland) overlooking the main beach at Dieppe. If they did not succeed the Canadians landing half an hour later, would be in big trouble.

Puys

The assault on Puys was given to the men of the Royal Regiment of Canada, supported by machine guns and mortars manned by the Black Watch of Canada and some light artillery. They would attack in two waves, 10 minutes apart. A third force would land to protect their flank.

They were to "secure the headland east of Jubilee (Dieppe) and destroy local objectives consisting of machine-gun posts, heavy and light flak installations and a 4 gun battery... and... protect an engineer demolition party operating in the gas works and power plant." It was a very ambitious plan for this small band of men.

The defences facing the Royals at Puys were formidable. The landing beach was very narrow and tall cliffs overlook the defile into the village. The Germans had sited a number of pillboxes on the cliffs and facing the beach (one was disguised as a Summer House). At the head of the beach was a 4 metre high sea wall. Heavy belts of barbed wire ran across the top of it.

"All in all , it would have been difficult to discover anywhere on the Coast of Europe, a less favourable area for an assault landing."
D.J. Goodspeed, Official Historian of the Royal Regiment of Canada.

Pourville

The assault on Pourville (4 km west of Dieppe) was the responsibility of the South Saskatchewan Regiment. The SSR was to push through the village and capture the cliffs overlooking Dieppe (West Headland). The Cameron Highlanders of Canada, who would land 30 minutes later, were to push beyond the village, occupy a German airfield, destroy a German Battery, then connect with some Canadian tanks from Dieppe and raid a German Headquarters 10 km south of Pourville. The tasks allotted to the Camerons were unrealistic. The timing and execution required to complete their objectives was far beyond the abilities of inexperienced troops and perhaps any troops.

Dieppe, The Main Assault

The main assault was to be launched at Dieppe by the Royal Hamilton Light Infantry, the Essex Scottish, and the 14th Canadian Army Tank Regiment (The Calgary Regiment) at 5:20 A.M. This was to be half an hour after the flank attacks had started and by which time the two headlands would be in Canadian hands. The Essex Scottish would land on the left ('Red' Beach) and the Royal Hamilton Light Infantry on the right ('White' Beach) along Dieppe's 1.6 km beach. The Calgary Tanks would land with the infantry to assist in both attacks. In reserve would be Les Fusiliers Mont-Royal, and the Royal Marine Commando. They had been assigned to capture and collect the invasion barges in the harbour of Dieppe and, if possible, sail them back to England.

The beach at Dieppe is overlooked by 45 metre-high cliffs. The beach itself is flat and open. It is stony (shingle), not sandy. The stones or chert are 5-10 cm in diameter and very slippery, especially when wet. The Germans had fortified the beach, cliffs and town with a variety of pillboxes, barbed wire, vehicle obstacles, and huge blockades. In addition a cement sea wall faced the beach and protected the Promenade from nature's fury. It served as another natural defensive barrier. The German garrison was at full strength, with plenty of supporting firepower. In addition the tide and weather conditions were right for a raid so the Garrison was also on "Alert".

The Raid on Dieppe

On the afternoon of Tuesday, August 18th, 1942 the attackers boarded their ships in the five ports and by 7 P.M. had been in place and given their orders. For the first time since the cancellation of "Rutter", they found out Dieppe was their official target. Maps and photographs were distributed to the men, and before nightfall the flotilla, 237 strong, was on its way. During the crossing there was a complete communications black-out. Surprise was the attackers' strongest weapon against the German defences, and radio communication could give their secret away. In the darkness the armada passed through an enemy minefield. All was going well.

Interception

At 3:47 A.M. a small German coastal patrol, consisting of eight small ships ran into the western flank of the flotilla. In a short fight one German ship was sunk and the rest dispersed. There was some damage to the escorting ships, but the real damage was the scattering of the vessels containing No.3 Commando destined for Bruneval.

The fight was so quick, that with the total communications silence, some thought the flashing and noise was the result of German guns firing from the coast. As the ships got closer to Dieppe no one understood what had happened. Twenty km from the French coast the infantry were lowered into the landing craft and the run for the beaches was on.

The Landings

The Commandos

The encounter with the German convoy had scattered the 23 ships, containing No.3 Commando, attacking Bruneval. None-the-less they managed to put seven shiploads ashore. The majority of the men were captured by the Germans, who out-numbered the Commandos about 4 to 1.

Another small party of 20 men managed to evade the Germans and get off the beach. They harassed the Germans at the coastal battery for a few hours, returned to the beach and to the flotilla.

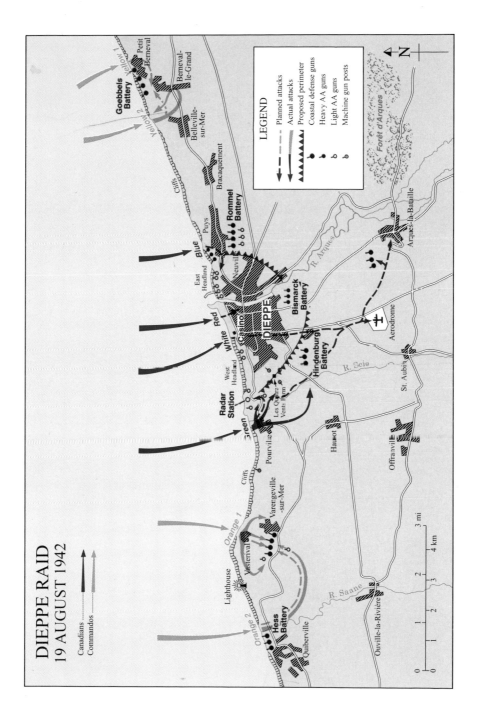

DIEPPE RAID
19 AUGUST 1942

Canadians ....
Commandos ....

LEGEND

Planned attacks
Actual attacks
Proposed perimeter
Coastal defense guns
Heavy AA guns
Light AA guns
Machine gun posts

N

Petit
Berneval
Goebbels
Battery
Berneval-
le-Grand
Yellow 1
Belleville-
sur-Mer
Yellow 2
Cliffs
Bracquement
Rommel
Battery
Blue
Puys
East
Headland
Neuville
DIEPPE
Casino
White
Red
West
Headland
Bismarck
Battery
Hindenburg
Battery
Radar
Station
Les Quatre
Vents Farm
Green
Pourville
Cliffs
Varengeville
-sur-Mer
Orange 1
Vasterival
Lighthouse
Orange 2
Hess
Battery
Quiberville
Ouville-la-Rivière
R. Saane

Forêt d'Arques
Arques-la-Bataille
R. Arques
Aerodrome
R. Scie
St. Aubin
Haubot
Offranville

0   1   2   3 mi
0   1   2   3   4 km

At Varengeville, No.4 Commando, attacking on the extreme west of the Raid, landed and executed their operation like a training exercise. They landed on schedule and split into two parties. One party fired at the Germans in the emplacement while the second circled around behind, and captured the position with the bayonet! The Commandos destroyed the guns, returned to the beach and then to the flotilla. They achieved all their objectives and suffered only 45 killed and wounded! If only the other landings could have gone as well.

Puys; The Eastern Flank Attack

At Puys surprise was crucial, and the Royals were 30 minutes late. Instead of hitting the beach under the cover of darkness, they landed in the early morning light. Instead of landing in advance of the main assault at Dieppe, they were landing after it. There was no surprise. As the landing craft carrying the first wave approached the shore, the Germans were waiting.

A storm of machine-gun fire greeted the leading boats. As the door of the LCAs lowered, the men were shot down before they could move. Soldiers were falling in heaps on the ramps of their landing craft, or dropping into the water. Others were killed as they leapt onto the beach. Dead and wounded were piling up on the shore. For those few men who escaped the withering crossfire, the only safety was at the foot of the sea wall 40 metres away. Only a handful made it.

Twenty minutes later the second wave approached the beach. German flares illuminated the skies, and the sounds of explosions and bullets cut the air. When the boats touched down they were greeted with the same murderous fire that had killed so many of the first wave. Many of the raiders leapt out of the landing craft into the water, and were forced to swim to shore under heavy fire. To have any hope of survival the Canadians had to run across to the Sea Wall.

"As I was walking off the landing craft I was actually walking over our own dead and wounded,... I got half way up the beach and dropped,...I looked around and there were men lying down ... I got up and ran and made it to the wall, and when I got to the wall and looked back and I said to myself, 'if they don't move, they're going get killed', and then I suddenly realized they couldn't move, they were already dead."
Ron Beal, Private, Royal Regiment of Canada

FAILURE AT PUYS 19 AUGUST 1942

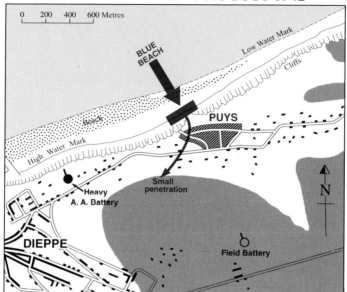

A third wave landed shortly after. They came ashore at the foot of the unscaleable cliffs, and were trapped. British fighter-bombers strafed the German positions as they continuously swept over the beach trying to provide cover for the pinned-down Canadians.

Along the Sea Wall a group of 20 Royals climbed over the wall at a spot where the barbed wire had been destroyed. The valiant men advanced up towards the top of the cliff, captured two German positions, and when surrounded, escaped into a nearby wood. Later in the afternoon, after the fighting had died down and there was no chance of evacuation, they surrendered.

"Is there any possible chance of getting us off?"
Message sent to the Fleet from Puys beach.

For the next hour the Germans continued firing at the men on the beach. They fired back but it was obvious the assault was over. On several occasions ships tried to get into shore to evacuate the survivors. The gallant sailors had little success against the terrific German fire, and many paid with their lives. Now stranded and desperately alone the Canadians at Puys surrendered. In two hours the Royals, who had started the attack with 554 men, were returning to England with only 65! The bodies of more than 200 of their comrades littered the shore, or lay huddled in death along the Sea Wall. Two hundred and eighty were now prisoners of war. For these men the Second World War lasted less than two hours!

As the fire slackened and Puys became quiet once more, the sound of heavy fighting could be heard coming over the cliffs - from Dieppe.

Pourville; The Western Flank Attack

The other Canadian flank attack went in at 4:52 A.M., right on time. The leading wave was the Prairie men of the South Saskatchewan Regiment. It appeared surprise in the dim light had been achieved as the Saskatchewans quickly pushed over the beach and entered the small village. However, the small German garrison had detected the raid and as the SSR entered the streets of Pourville they were met with heavy fire.

The enemy was well-entrenched on the slopes leading up to the West Headland, and from these positions, stopped the advance. The Saskatchewans, after fighting through Pourville, were faced with crossing the Scie River (they were supposed to have landed east of the river, but in the darkness, had disembarked on the wrong side) to get at the Germans. The fully loaded soldiers could not easily cross the open water and were forced to go over a small bridge just east of the village. The German defenders focussed their fire on the bridge and the South Saskatchewans were shot down in a hail of bullets.

"Come on boys, they can't hit a thing. Come on, let's go and get 'em."
Cecil Merritt, Commanding Officer, South Saskatchewan Regiment
(on crossing the bridge over the Scie River under heavy fire)

Their Commanding Officer, Cecil Merritt, took charge of the attack, and walking calmly onto the bridge waved his men forward. Sensing his courage and seemingly incredible luck, the Saskatchewans stormed across the bridge and captured the German positions. They were still a long way from the West Headland, and had lost valuable time in getting across the Scie. The lost time cost them dearly, as Nazi reinforcements joined in the battle and their advance was stopped.

In the meantime the Cameron Highlanders of Canada had landed shortly after the Saskatchewans. They were supposed to pass through the captured village and race on to seize the airfield several km distant. As the fighting was still going on when they arrived, they quickly joined in the attack. Trying to keep to their plan the Camerons pushed three km inland but ran into a fierce German defence. The tanks that were to assist them had not arrived from Dieppe. With no hope of continuing the Highlanders staged a fighting withdrawal back to Pourville. With enemy forces closing in and the two Canadian regiments fighting for their lives, the evacuation commenced.

The courage shown by the sailors of the Royal Navy was incredible as they faced a tornado of German fire approaching the beach. Fearlessly they came to the aid of the stranded Canadians. More than half of the men at Pourville were evacuated. Only the dead and a small rearguard remained. This small group offered a ferocious defence and discouraged the attacking Germans, thus buying valuable time for the evacuation. The majority of these men were taken prisoners and amongst their number was Cecil Merritt.

By 1:37 P.M. Pourville was back in German hands. Of the 523 Saskatchewans who had embarked on the Raid, 81 had been killed, 193 wounded and 92 taken prisoner. The Camerons lost 243 out of 503, including 68 dead.

The worst tragedy in the failure of both flank attacks was not the losses in men, but that they did not achieve their primary goals. They failed to capture the Headlands overlooking the Dieppe beach. They failed to protect the flanks of the frontal assault on Dieppe. The "boys" would be sitting ducks.

Dieppe; The Main Attack

As the landing craft carrying the two regiments of infantry and tanks approached the shore the sounds of battle could be heard from Pourville. The guns from four Royal Navy destroyers were firing on Dieppe. Swarms of Royal Air Force fighter-bombers were sweeping over the cliffs and Dieppe itself, harassing the German defenders and covering the approaching ships.

At 5:20 A.M., right on time, the landing craft lowered their ramps and the Canadians raced onward, towards the beach. The Germans met their attackers with a fierce fire. Men tumbled forward. Many fell, some having

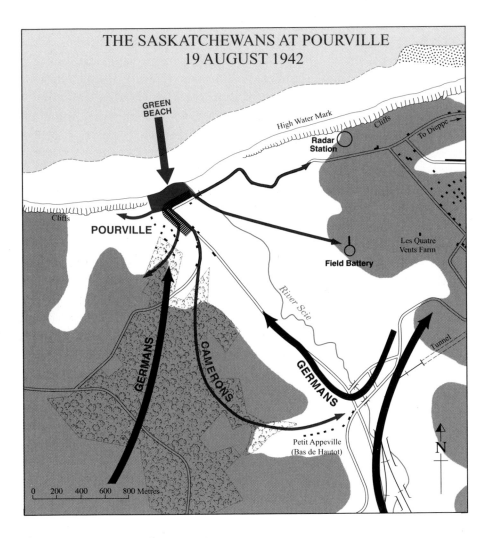

THE SASKATCHEWANS AT POURVILLE
19 AUGUST 1942

GREEN
BEACH

High Water Mark

Cliffs

Radar
Station

To Dieppe

Cliffs

POURVILLE

Les Quatre
Vents Farm

Field Battery

River Scie

GERMANS

CAMERONS

GERMANS

Tunnel

Petit Appeville
(Bas de Hautot)

N

0   200   400   600   800 Metres

lost their footing on the stony shore, and others being killed in the hail of bullets. The noise was deafening.

The Essex Scottish were responsible for the attack on the eastern section of the beach or "Red Beach". As the infantry left the assault craft they were hit by a pelting storm of bullets and explosions. They may not have noticed it at the time but the Germans were shooting at them from the overlooking cliffs of the East Headland. It was clear the attack at Puys had not reached its objective. Their most immediate concern was to find a defence against the over-whelming intensity of the Nazi firepower. They should have been supported by the Calgary tanks but they had not arrived. The aircraft had departed, leaving them an unprotected 100 metre run across the beach, before they could get some decent cover. The German machine-guns swept the beach cutting down the attackers. None-the-less some of the courageous Scottish made it across to the Sea Wall but were pinned down and could go no further. The enemy used their high trajectory mortars to lob death on the Canadians even as they hugged the wall for their very lives.

On the western section of the beach or "White Beach" the Royal Hamilton Light Infantry landed. They were greeted with a hail of fire but the RHLI was not daunted. They cut their way through the beach obstacles and quickly crossed the beach. The Germans were defending "White Beach" with a series of pillboxes, and an abandoned Casino. The RHLI fought to capture the pillboxes and after a vicious action, cleared the enemy. They next took the Casino and small groups advanced into Dieppe itself. This had been accomplished without support, because the tanks had not arrived. Where the Hell were the tanks?

"I landed on the gravel and ran up the beach. The noise was indescribable; rifle fire, machine gun fire from both sides, and shells being lobbed over ...I also remember seeing, like a heavy rain on a mill pond, the bullets splashing the water. And it was blood red. And bodies floating around ...our buddies were being killed..."
Al Comfort, Corporal, Royal Hamilton Light Infantry

Finally the first landing craft carrying the Churchill tanks of the Calgary Regiment, arrived 15 minutes late. Nine of the 39 tonne tanks were to be involved in the first attack, but when they reached shore the Germans focussed a torrent of fire on them, putting two out of action and

(CWM 12276)

Dieppe Raid by Carles Comfort.

THE DIEPPE ASSAULT 19 AUGUST 1942

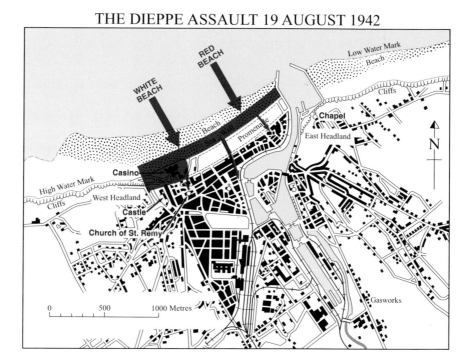

Dieppe beaches under fire.

(PAC 183791)

damaging others. Gradually ten landing craft carrying 30 tanks came ashore and 27 of the tanks entered the battle. Sadly, two tanks, with their crews, were landed in deep water and were "drowned".

The tanks immediately started firing to support the infantry, then rumbled forward, the large stones on the beach causing their caterpillar treads to slip, and in some cases getting trapped in the mechanism and immobilizing the tank.

"You couldn't pick worse terrain for a tracked vehicle. You turn the vehicle a little bit, the stones are rolled into the track, and if you get too many going through at once you break your track."
Allan Glenn, Major, Calgary Tank Regiment

The sight of the tanks must have greatly cheered the soldiers. Their plodding advance towards the old port, made it seem the tide had turned. Of the tanks that survived the beach, half made it to the Sea Wall, and over. They appeared to be on their way to link up with the Camerons from Pourville. But on this day nothing would go the Canadians' way. The leading streets into Dieppe had been blocked by massive concrete obstacles, and there was no way for the Calgarians to get through. These courageous men did all in their power to reach their objectives, but without the capability to destroy the road blocks there was nothing they could do. They gradually returned to the beach, looking to be evacuated, or to help the others trapped there with some covering fire. It had been their first action in their new tanks and it had not gone well.

The attack had been on for a little over one hour and already it seemed doomed. On "Red Beach" the Essex Scottish were pinned down. Small parties did attack over the Sea Wall but could make no progress against the fierce fire and solid defences. The tanks had struggled forward but could do no more. Little groups of the RHLI were fighting in Dieppe itself, but it was clear the Germans could not be pushed out. The East and West Headlands were both clearly in enemy hands. Perhaps it was time to get out of there, and withdraw the remnants of the attacking force. The men, huddled on the beach for safety, still fired back at the Germans in Dieppe and on the cliffs. They had held on for 100 minutes of Hell. The bodies of their friends lay prostrate on the pebbled beach or bobbed on the shoreline. Wounded soldiers were everywhere. Smoke of burning tanks and vehicles

The wreck of "Blossom" in front of the Casino. It was put out of action when it broke its right track on the chert. The entire crew was captured.
(H. Henry Collection, Bundes archive 362220722)

The wreck of "Burns" in front of the Sea Wall. The tank was put out of action when shell fire blew off its right track. One of the crew was killed. The others were taken prisoner.
(H. Henry Collection, DAA 2815 08 407028)

mingled with the explosions from mortars and artillery. The men could see approaching boats. Would it be their chance to get away?

The Approaching Boats

As the line of landing craft hit the beaches, they lowered their ramps, but instead of being empty, ready to take on survivors, they were loaded with fresh troops coming to reinforce the attack. Even the Germans must have been surprised.

Due to poor communication and conflicting reports the Canadian general in command of the assault had ordered in his reserves to exploit a perceived but non-existent success on "Red Beach". The soldiers of the Fusiliers Mont-Royal must have accepted their assignment with great trepidation.

While approaching the shore the Germans focussed their fire on them, and although they were spread out along the shoreline they could not escape the shells. As they poured out of the boats many were shot down, but regardless of the danger they raced across the beach and joined their comrades of the Essex Scottish and the RHLI. A few made it into Dieppe but the majority could do little but take cover. One group landed opposite the steep cliffs and could not even get to the cover of the Sea Wall.

"As soon as we came out from underneath the smoke screen, we thought there would be a liberated beach, but we came in and the first thing we saw was the town hall in flames, and we moved forward, ... everyone was being killed ...it was a massacre..."
Paul Duman, Corporal, Fusilier Mont-Royal

"It was like a big storm, a big thunder storm, tracer bullets coming from everywhere and bombs and everything, and you could smell the burning flesh,... I remember the water being kinda pinkish,... everybody, including myself, were praying, and calling for our mother ...we were stuck there, and you see all those dead bodies, and see sometimes somebody wounded but still walking, but with their guts hanging out and their arms cut off,..."
Raymond Geoffrian, Private, Fusilier Mont-Royal

At 8 A.M. a second wave of reinforcements, the British Royal Marines, "A" Commando, was sent in, based on another erroneous report. It was believed the tanks were progressing well and the Casino and beach were in Canadian hands. The Marines were met with a withering fire from the

(CWM 14424)

Casualties on the Beach by A. Hierl.

Germans and many were killed. Their Commanding Officer was shot trying to wave off the trailing landing craft. He had realized what fate awaited his men and had died trying to save them. They became just another group to be stranded or killed on the stony Dieppe shingle.

It was now after 8:00 A.M. and it was clear the Raid had failed. The beach itself was a shambles. The men were continuously under German fire and with each passing minute more and more of the attackers were being killed. For the Germans it was a turkey shoot. The surviving tanks nobly fired back, relying on their armour-plating for protection.

On the beach the wounded were being tended to as best the medics could do. Many, in the face of certain death, went to the aid of their suffering comrades. John Foote, Chaplain of the RHLI was particularly fearless in giving aid to the wounded. He repeatedly crossed the beach to bring back wounded men, constantly putting his life at risk. For many he was an Angel of Mercy.

The Withdrawal

By 9:00 A.M., less than four hours after the landing, it was finally clear to those in command that "Jubilee" had become solely an operation to save as many of those trapped on the beach as possible. At 11:00 A.M., with the assistance of fighter-bombers, and with as much Naval artillery as was available, the first boats approached the beaches. The Germans had waited for the evacuation and they rained steel and explosives on the

---

"A lot of fellas, hundreds of them, decided they were going to swim out... you could see bodies twitch as the snipers were hitting them... they (the Germans) dropped myriads of these tiny little bombs... and they started exploding and there were parts of bodies flying up.. A good six or eight feet along the water's edge was just bodies and parts of bodies floating there."
Geoffrey Ellwood, Private, Royal Canadian Corps of Signals

---

incoming vessels. At "Red Beach" six of eight boats were sunk. But the courage of the men of the Royal Navy could not be denied and attempt after attempt was made to reach the shore. As a boat came close to shore survivors made mad dashes to get on board and the Germans sitting atop the over-hanging cliffs peppered the boats, turning the water into a boiling cauldron. The efforts to evacuate continued for the next two hours, each

Dieppe, August 19th, 1942.   (PAC C17293)

Prisoners of War, Dieppe, August 19th, 1942.   (PAC C14171)

ship taking its turn and coming into shore, firing salvoes at the German positions and trying to cover an escape from the shore. On the shingle the last of the Calgary tanks was still firing, but by 1:10 P.M. it was no longer possible for the boats to reach the beach. Just before 2:00 P.M. the German guns fell silent. The Raid on Dieppe was over.

Aftermath

For all the effort only a small number of men were rescued from the Dieppe beaches. Of the 553 members of the Essex Scottish which had embarked for the Raid only 50 made it home. The remainder were killed (121) or captured (382). The Royal Hamilton Light Infantry faired slightly better. More than 200 were saved from the beach, but sadly, 197 were killed and 175 were taken prisoner. Of the 316 Royal Canadian Engineers who accompanied the Dieppe attack only a handful made it back to England.

The Allied flotilla carrying the survivors returned to England without mishap. It had started out carrying 4,963 Canadians and returned with only 2,210, of whom 1,000 had not even landed. Of the men who did land 1,874 were taken prisoner and 907 were killed. Seventy percent of the Canadians who landed never returned from the Raid! This is only a statistic. Before long homes all across Canada, but particularly in Montreal, Toronto, Hamilton and Windsor, would receive the dreaded telegrams, telling them that their son or husband or father was dead. Statistics can never tell of the immense grief felt in those homes after the 19th August 1942.

On the beach itself the survivors lay amid the dead as the Germans cautiously approached the smoking ruins. Amongst the three thousand Canadian soldiers were close to 600 wounded and 900 corpses. The remains of 27 tanks, smoking landing craft and dozens of other vehicles lay scattered and quiet. For the Germans it had been an enormous and easy victory. At a cost of less than 600 casualties and several thousand shells they had smashed an armada and an attacking force of 5,000 men. They could not be more pleased with their performance. The Germans surveyed the beach and confidently predicted that the Allies were no match for their defences.

The victors began their task of rounding up the prisoners, and organizing the wounded, but much of that would wait while they posed for souvenir photographs beside the wrecked tanks and the dead. These photographs would later be turned into effective propaganda by the victorious Germans. They collected the tired and bloodied prisoners and paraded them through the streets of Dieppe, a humiliating experience for those courageous men.

Amongst the 2,000 Canadian captives were Lieutenant-Colonel Cecil Merritt, taken at Pourville and Chaplain John Foote, the valiant Padre of the Royal Hamilton Light Infantry. Both men were awarded the Victoria Cross, the British Empire's highest award for bravery, for their heroic actions on August 19th, 1942.

Later the dead were removed from Dieppe, Pourville and Puys and taken to a location south of the Port, where they were buried with full military honours. They rest there today. The Maple Leaf is engraved on their Portland headstones. It is a lonely place, a place no living Canadian reached that day.

Dieppe; An Analysis

Shortly after the return to England the debate over the value and meaning of the Raid started. Reputations were at stake and it was clear the people did not want to hear of another disaster. The immediate response was that it was, in fact, a success. Flashy headlines told the public of this dramatic and daring raid that left the Germans "very badly rattled". It was, however, impossible to hide the long list of casualties from their families across Canada, and before long the Canadian public was demanding answers. One Canadian newspaper went so far as to blame the disaster on the "bankruptcy" of Canadian Generalship.

"For many a day there were sad duties to perform. The few possessions of those who had gone were piled in little heaps, listed and despatched. Casualty states were prepared, showing the known dead, the wounded, the missing. And then there were the letters. These came in daily to the Regiment, asking what had happened to husbands, friends, and sweethearts. All had to be answered."
D.J. Goodspeed, Official Historian of the Royal Regiment of Canada.

It was at this time, in 1942, that the controversy about the Dieppe Raid took form. There were (and still are) two basic views. The first supports the contention that Dieppe was a good thing, and that the lessons learned were crucial to the success of the D-Day Landings in 1944.

The second view was that Dieppe was a disaster, a poorly planned and poorly executed operation. Its purpose had been to satisfy the ego, ambition and enthusiasm of the higher-ups. To the critics of the Raid the only reason the first view exists is to cover the behinds of those involved in its conception and execution.

A variety of quotes on the following pages illustrate the complexity and passion of the two views.

That the Raid had not succeeded (it was called a non-success by one Canadian General) in its military objectives could not be in dispute. With the exception of one of the Commando attacks, no one had come even close to reaching the objectives planned for them on August 19th.

"Although at the time the heavy cost to Canada, and the non-success of the Dieppe operation seemed hard to bear, I believe that when this war is examined in proper perspective, it will be seen that the sobering influence of that operation on existing Allied strategical conceptions, with the enforced realization by the Allied Governments of the lengthy and tremendous preparations necessary before invasion could be attempted, was a Canadian contribution of the greatest significance to final victory."
Harry Crerar, General Commanding the Canadian Army in Europe, 1943.

It was clear that the Raid did not politically satisfy the Russians, who still wanted a Second Front, nor did it help the morale of the general population. It was just another failure to them. Perhaps the civilian population most positively affected by the Raid were the French. Although they were not liberated they now knew they had not been forgotten. Sooner or later the invasion would come.

The Raid had brought Canadian troops some much needed action, but at such an enormous cost, that it had shaken Canadian confidence. Amongst the Canadians "it was not only unchivalrous, but unpatriotic to criticize Dieppe", but "misgivings about the Canadian Army had crept in after Dieppe".

"Dieppe, in retrospect, looks so recklessly hare-brained an enterprise that it is difficult to reconstruct the official state of mind which gave it birth and drove it forward."
John Keagan, British Military Historian

So why did Dieppe fail?

The Dieppe plan was seriously flawed. The planners did not provide sufficient fire support for the attacking troops. The fact that the planners did not see the need for a heavy bombardment to destroy German defensive emplacements meant they underestimated the strength of the enemy's positions. This oversight was fatal. The Nazis were far too well entrenched and protected to be harmed by the type of bombardment used against them in advance of the landing. German positions were not damaged or knocked out, and once the artillery stopped shooting and the fighter-bombers stopped strafing, all they had to do was go to their machine-guns and shoot down the Canadians who were by now moving in the open, across the beaches.

The Tank support plan which was supposed to help the infantry was also flawed. For the tanks to properly assist the men they had to arrive exactly at the same time after crossing 100 km of the English Channel. Any miscalculations would hurt the timing of the landings and jeopardize the assault. This plan was too rigid and impossible to execute. It also did not adequately solve the problems of the shingle, the concrete obstacles, or the Sea Wall.

The idea of the flanking attacks was also too complex and too rigid. If either of the flanking attacks failed the main assault would be at risk. Once again the planners had designed an operation that was inflexible and which would be almost impossible to accomplish.

Other parts of the plan, such as linking the tanks from Dieppe with the Camerons from Pourville to assault a German position 10 km away, then returning to the beach for evacuation, landing the Royal Marine Commandos to capture barges in the Port and sail them back to England (so they could find out what short of foodstuffs the French were getting!), are simply ludicrous.

So we know the planning for Dieppe was severely flawed, too inflexible, and lacking sufficient firepower and resources. Why then, did no one stop the Raid?.

Who was responsible?

Trying to lay blame for the Dieppe Raid has been a full-time preoccupation for historians since 1942. It is difficult to do because so many Generals, Admirals and Air Marshals were involved in the committee

(CWM 14422)

Mopping up after the battle by F.M. Lunstroth.

work leading up to the attack. It is hard to determine who, what, when and where. It appears that everyone thought someone else was looking after the planning details. Even today it is not clear whether the British Prime Minister, Winston Churchill or the Chief of the Combined Operations, Lord Louis Mountbatten, was responsible for mounting the operation. Mountbatten is usually considered the main force behind the Raid, and therefore the focus of criticism. But it is clear that many could have and should have contested the plan. This includes Canadian Generals.

Although the Canadians were enthusiastic about getting into action in 1942 not all Canadians were keen on this sort of Raid. Many had fought in the First World War and had experienced the problems associated with frontal attacks on fortified positions. These men were in the minority.

"...the bigger raids such as... the Dieppe raid I was all against. I couldn't see that any lessons could be learnt which couldn't be learnt from the study of past experiences... or that it might gain any experience which was really worthwhile, which you couldn't foresee... I was anxious enough to get into battle - but I was thankful my division wasn't asked to go to Dieppe - but my views were well known."
General George Pearkes, V.C., First Canadian Division, 1942.

For the most part the Canadian Generals had backed the Dieppe Raid and were stung by the criticism from Canada. They became defensive. The standard fall-back became the official line - that the lessons learned at Dieppe contributed significantly to victory. By taking this view Dieppe could be seen officially as a success not a failure. It was still a hot spot, a topic not to be mentioned.

"(Canadian General) Worthington concluded the talk by warning me that I should avoid criticism or even discussion of the operation, because this would not be at all popular with the higher-ups."
General E.L.M.Burns, Second Canadian Division, 1943.

The lessons of Dieppe became the official line and is still the only reasonable justification for the Raid. The chief proponent of "Dieppe as a good thing", Lord Louis Mountbatten, was the Commander of Combined Operations, and the one mainly responsible for the Raid. Lord Louis assured the public (to his dying day) that what was learnt in the Dieppe Raid was critical in developing the strategy for the invasion of Europe that took place in 1944. Knowledge about the German defences, amphibious landings, planning and tactics that could not be learned in any other way, but through trial and error, were obtained from this sacrifice. So the men did not die in vain.

"It is impossible to overestimate the value of Dieppe. It was the turning point in the technique of invasion. Many vital lessons were learned... For every man who died at Dieppe in 1942, at least ten or more must have been spared in the invasion of Normandy in 1944."
Lord Louis Mountbatten,
Vice-Admiral, Chief of Combined Operations, 1942

So what were these important lessons they were always referring to?

The "Lessons learned" from Dieppe were numerous, but the principal ones included: overwhelming fire support, including close support is needed during the initial stages of the attack; assaults should be planned to develop around the flanks of a strongly defended locality rather than frontally against it; air cover is important in the success of an amphibious landing; the attacks should be flexible and not requiring precision timing; and landings should not take place in daylight. There were also many recommendations with respect to the training of an amphibious force. There should be a permanent naval assault force set up just for these operations. There was much discussion about the type of equipment required to complement the infantry force in an amphibious landing. There were many more "Lessons" but these were the major conclusions drawn from the Dieppe Raid. All were valid, but many felt the planners should have known them before the Raid took place. Even the Official Canadian historian admitted the "lessons were not new".

Probably the most important lesson was brought about by the sobering effect of the Dieppe failure. The planners would never again be over-confident. There could be no illusions after Dieppe.

"That much-criticized undertaking had made an essential contribution to the success of the most momentous operation of war ever attempted."
"An uncovenanted result of the Dieppe raid was thus to warp the Germans' system of defence in North-West Europe to our advantage."
C.P. Stacey Official Historian of the Canadian Army

The grave of Private Kenneth Ingram of Toronto, killed in action August 19th, 1942, in Dieppe Canadian War Cemetery, France. His brother, Robert, was killed two years later and now shares his brother's grave. (N. Christie)

"That raid (Dieppe), carried out by a strong force of Canadians, had resulted in a high percentage of losses. From it we learned a number of lessons that we later applied to our advantage, but the price paid by the Canadians still rankled."
Dwight D. Eisenhower, Supreme Commander of all Allied Forces in Europe.

"I decided then that those who planned this disaster had to be idiots."
Jack A. Poolton, Captured at Dieppe, Royal Regiment of Canada.

The "Lessons" argument was supported by men holding senior positions, but found much criticism from many others. The view of those who disagreed with the official line was that the lessons of Dieppe were obvious and well known before the Raid and were strictly a cover-up for incompetence. There can be no doubt this was true. In fact some felt it was the Germans who learned the lessons from all the captured material, including the new Churchill tanks, which were left on the beaches after the Raid. As more details of the Raid surfaced, gradually the official argument started to lose its shine.

"This is the first time that the British have had the courtesy to cross the sea to offer the enemy a complete sample of their weapons.'
Adolf Hitler

"When the real facts of what had happened at Dieppe began to be known, there was a certain amount of discussion among officers who were veterans of World War I about the soundness of the tactics which had been adopted."
General E.L.M. Burns, Second Canadian Division, 1943.

Probably the best way to see Dieppe is as a difficult operation launched at a difficult time in the war. It was a time when there were equipment shortages and many inexperienced Generals and soldiers, a time of desperation. Within that framework we can understand what happened here. It is probably safe to say that whatever lessons learned they were not worth the loss of lives, but to the credit of the planners they did not make those mistakes again. The next time they would get it right. Next time the Germans would also be thinking of Dieppe, and in the erratic mind of Adolf Hitler, his decisions based on Dieppe would result in great opportunities for the Allies in Normandy in 1944.

These unique photographs were taken by Jack Handley of the Royal Regiment of Canada. He used a home-made pinhole camera made in a German Prisoner-of-War Camp. Canadian POWs were tied or shackled for more than 400 days in 1942-43 in retaliation for the tying of the hands of German POWs captured in raids on the French coast in 1942.

(Tim Stewart Collection)

"I believe that we could have got the information and experience we needed without losing so many magnificent Canadian soldiers."
Field-Marshall B. Montgomery, Commanding all British and Canadian Forces in Europe, 1944-45.

"They will get the thrashing of their lives"... "I am convinced that when the time comes it (the Landing) will be a huge relief, just like Dieppe."
Adolf Hitler, on the anticipated Allied Landing in France, 1944

After all is said and done and the bickering between the sides is discounted we are left with the tragedy and sacrifice on the beaches of Dieppe, Pourville and Puys. If we think the lessons learned through the deaths of more than 900 Canadians were not worth the cost, did these men die in vain?

In the context of the Second World War, the loss of 900 men in a War that claimed tens of millions of lives, seems almost insignificant. There were many, many great tragedies in the Second World War, Dieppe was but a small one. Within a few months the Allies had successfully landed in North Africa, the Russians had stalled the Nazis in the East, even the tide was turning against the Japanese. The tide of war had changed. Before long it would be Adolf Hitler's armies on the run.

So did they die in vain? During the Second World War a million Canadian men and women selflessly chose to enlist. They chose to risk their lives to stop the most evil tyrant the world had ever seen. They chose to put everything on the line to stop a vile man, a murderer of millions of children. It took their great courage, and the courage of millions like them, to defeat Adolf Hitler. Along the way there were tragedies like Dieppe. They did not die in vain, their sacrifices saved millions of lives. They were heroes.

The Greatest Air Battle of the War

At dawn on August 19th, 1942 the pilots and crew of more than 65 squadrons of the Royal Air Force (RAF) and the Royal Canadian Air Force (RCAF) waited at their bases across southern England. More than 750 aircraft were ready to participate in what became the greatest air battle of the Second World War. Their targets were the beaches and headlands surrounding the French seaport of Dieppe.

Most of the squadrons were fighters; speedy Spitfires or Hawker Hurricanes or Typhoons. There were also five squadrons of medium bombers; Bostons and Blenheim bombers. Neither were considered good aircraft. These were out-dated aircraft, too slow and often more of a danger to their crews than the Germans.

They were ordered to provide air cover for the flotilla of ships carrying the Raiders across the English Channel, attack the German coastal defences around Dieppe, lay a smoke screen to cover the landing troops, and then cover the evacuation and the return of the convoy to England.

But they had another goal; to draw-out and destroy all German aircraft they encountered. They would, once and for all, determine who dominated the air war over the Channel and the coast of France. These were ambitious objectives.

Shortly after dawn hundreds of Spitfires left the English coast, flying just above sea level, for the shores of Dieppe. Before the day was over more than 1,000 planes would be involved in the air battle. One hundred and fifty would be destroyed.

In small groups the Spitfires swept over the German defences, machine-gunning any visible targets. German ground fire was severe and the planes were so close to the ground they could see the faces of the Nazis. Through the smoke and fire the Spits flashed over the chalk cliffs of Dieppe. Others dropped smoke bombs on the beaches as the landing craft moved quickly towards the shore. The fighters swept once more over the beaches firing at the German positions, but they could not damage the well-constructed concrete bunkers that housed the enemy's most powerful guns. With their ammunition and fuel running low and the infantry now on the beaches, the fighters returned to England to rearm and refuel. Their work was not finished and soon they would be back.

The beaches were now covered with Canadian troops running forward, some falling as a murderous fire swept the shingle. The covering fighters could do little to help for they could easily shoot their own men, but they did what they could to protect the Canadians.

Shortly after the troops landed, the German fighters accompanied by bombers, made their first appearance. They engaged the Spitfires and in a swirl of fire and smoke the air battle began in earnest. Before long more than 260 German fighters were battering the RAF and RCAF flyers. Planes were being shot down at an alarming rate. They would smoke then spin as they crashed into the sea at 300 km per hour. The German bombers flew directly for the ships of the convoy, but were intercepted by the Spitfires. More than 120 German Dornier bombers would attack the vessels and bomb the landing craft on the beaches. The fighters swarmed about the slower bombers and several quickly went down in flames. It was critical that the Germans be kept away from the flotilla. Ultimately 24 Dorniers would be destroyed, but the Spitfires were paying a price as dozens were shot down in the swirl of battle by the German Luftwaffe's Foche-Wulf and Messerschmitt fighters. Ground fire was also taking its toll of the Spits.

By the early afternoon, as the evacuation started, the RAF and RCAF fighters flew low over the beaches dropping more smoke bombs to cover the retreating troops. The pilots fearlessly flew low over the German positions risking instant death from the anti-aircraft guns. Others were still engaged against the German bombers, as they tried to drop bombs on the waiting ships.

Finally when no more men could be saved from the burning inferno on the beaches, the convoy turned for home, still protected by their fighter umbrella. The Luftwaffe chased them home but gained no opportunity to sink any of the ships of the Royal Navy. As they neared the English coast the Germans broke off their attack and returned to their bases in France. The greatest air battle of the war was over.

The RCAF and RAF lost 99 aircraft (mostly Spitfires) and 51 aircrew (mostly pilots) killed. Seventeen were taken prisoner. The German Luftwaffe had 48 planes destroyed and 24 damaged. They had lost 15% of their force, losses the Germans could not afford.

In all the Allied planes had flown 2600 sorties, an average of more than three trips per aircraft. They had fought with courage and had protected the ships from destruction. They had performed their duties well and proved their domination of the Luftwaffe over the English Channel.

CANADIAN PACIFIC
TELEGRAPHS
World Wide Communications

CANADIAN PACIFIC
COMMUNICATIONS

W.D.NEIL. GENERAL MANAGER OF COMMUNICATIONS. MONTREAL.

C.D. 1R

WAA19 26/23 GB NL 2 EI REPORT DELY

OTTAWA ONT 23   1942 AUG 24 AM 2 60

MRS AUDRIE TUCKER 2123

96 BARTON AVE TORONTO

5749 SINGERELY REGRET INFORM YOU 367324 PRIVATE HARRY GEORGE

TUCKER OFFICIALLY REPORTED MISSING IN ACTION STOP FURTHER

INFORMATION FOLLOWS WHEN RECEIVED

OFFICER I/C RECORDS

Telegram received by Mrs. Harry G. Tucker of Toronto. Her husband was missing in the Puys attack. Private Tucker later listed as "killed." His body was never found.
(Tim Stewart Collection)

MK

Bibliography - Suggested Reading

Destined To Survive; A Dieppe Veteran's Story by Jack A. Poolton. Dundurn Press, 1998.

Dieppe, Tragedy To Triumph by Denis and Shelagh Whitaker. McGraw-Hill Ryerson, 1992.

Unauthorized Action, Mountbatten and the Dieppe Raid by Brian Loring Villa. Oxford University Press, 1990.

The Canadian Army, 1939-1945 by Colonel C.P. Stacey. King's Printer, 1948.

Six Armies in Normandy by John Keagan. The Viking Press, 1982.

A Nation Forged in Fire by J.L. Granatstein and Desmond Morton. Lester & Orpen Dennys Limited, 1989.

In Enemy Hands by Daniel G. Dancocks. Hurtig Press, 1983.

Battle Royal by D.J. Goodspeed. The Royal Regiment of Canada Association, 1962.

Where the Hell Are the Guns? by George G. Blackburn. McClelland & Stewart, 1997.